MY FAITH

Pat Boone Anita Bryant James Stewart
Billy Graham Johnny Cash Norman Vincent Peale
Glen Campbell Marjorie Holmes Lawrence Welk
Doris Day Eugenia Price Hal Lindsey
Dale Evans Rogers

compiled by Roger Elwood

designed by Wulf Stapelfeldt

The C. R. Gibson Company, Publishers

ABOUT THIS BOOK

Celebrities have to face life the same as non-celebrities, and while circumstances may vary, life's problems are often the same. The business of the celebrity is show business, a profession which tends not to engender deeply religious values. So much depends upon materialistic pursuits that spiritual matters may be given little or no consideration.

But there are exceptions to this practice among the scores of celebrities whose names appear in New York and Hollywood columns, as well as on television and motion picture screens. Not *everyone* is pursuing the "things of this world" to the exclusion of the spiritual values taught so clearly by Jesus Christ. Some are more vocal about their faith than others but all who are sincere find Christianity an integral part of their lives.

Pat Boone is a good example. As a pop singer and film star, he rose rapidly to the top of the ladder of success. His fans numbered into the hundreds of thousands, perhaps millions. And he was a Christian when he began his rise to popularity. For a time, he seemed content to subordinate his Christian witness to his efforts for stardom. But over the past three or four years, all of this has changed. Pat is more openly devoted to Christ than ever before, giving continuing witness to how a true Christian's life *must* be led.

Doris Day is another Christian celebrity. Certainly one of the highest paid stars in history, she nevertheless had little peace in her personal and spiritual life, going from one form of belief to another, until she said, "Lord, take control. I am Yours. Show me what You would have me do." Today, as a result, she is content, with the inner turmoil of many years no longer dominating her.

Johnny Cash's testimony could hardly be more indicative. He nearly destroyed himself through the consumption of pep pills and other drugs. Finally, as he was hitting bottom, he looked to God for help. Johnny found help and to date he has never once gone back to the drugs that enslaved him.

Jimmy Stewart is one of the quieter Christians in Hollywood. He hasn't said a great deal about the Christian way because he prefers to let his conduct speak for itself. And speak it has. There is no one in movie-making who has less than the greatest respect and affection for Jimmy — and many feel genuine love for this man.

Much of what has been said about Pat Boone, Doris Day, Johnny Cash and Jimmy Stewart could also be said about Eugenia Price, Billy Graham, Hal Lindsey, Glen Campbell, Dale Evans Rogers, Norman Vincent Peale, Marjorie Holmes, Anita Bryant and Lawrence Welk. Not all of these are in show business but all can be considered celebrities in that they are known to millions of people.

MY FAITH allows the reader to share and understand the thoughts of these celebrities on a variety of subjects, such as how to face crisis, what is true happiness, the meaning of love, the proper management of money, and others which offer insight for everyday living. The direct quotations in MY FAITH have been put together in a single book for the first time, and offer an opportunity for rare enlightenment and rich blessing.

ROGER ELWOOD

CONTENTS

BELIEF

Worshiping God in everything we do, walking with Him, or
being in union with Him, means that *He is with us wherever
we go*. We are in contact with Christ. This is the best way to
find out what a Christian can and cannot do. We don't need
religious laws to live by! We have God living in us, and He
is alive, so He will let you know beyond the shadow of any
doubt *if* you will listen to Him, whether or not He is happy
at the party or the entertainment to which the *two of you*
have gone together! Just because you choose to disobey Him
and go someplace where He would not feel "at home," does
not mean that God *stays* at home! He goes right with you.
And every few minutes, He will press against your heart and
your heart will ache because you know His Heart aches
over your disobedience. Walking with Him simply means
living with Him.

EUGENIA PRICE

The Jesus Revolution is the best thing that's happened to
America this century . . . There was a great need in the
United States for a spiritual revival, because the whole
country was becoming too materialistic.

JOHNNY CASH

Unless our belief in God causes us to help our fellowman, our
faith stands condemned. Our love for God is best proved by
our regard for the needs of our neighbors.

REV. BILLY GRAHAM

We live only once on this earth, so far as we know, and then we are gone on to a greater life. But here, by the grace of God, we have the priceless gift of just so many days and years, in which we are to do the best we can. We never know exactly how much time we have; for some it is a few days and years, for others it is many. It is in God's hands. But what time we have, we ought to have sense enough to use well. That's plain common sense.

DALE EVANS ROGERS

A person's whole future, his whole sense of identity, belonging and purpose may never become clear until he starts with his spiritual growth. There isn't any other way to become a sound individual, to learn to love where we have hated, to replace fear with confidence, to erase doubt with faith.

PAT BOONE

God wants us to be continually *filled* with the Spirit. The only way we can have this happen is to decide who runs the show in our lives. We need to make a once-for-all decision to give the title deed of our lives to God. This does not mean that we are always going to do what God wants us to do. It does mean that we have come to a point in life where we have soberly assessed what God has done for us in Christ. We reason that if He has given us eternal life, put us into His forever family, given us an inheritance with His Son, and made us kings and priests forever, then we can say with confidence, "I can trust a God like that. If I give my life totally into His keeping, He will know how to handle it and do the best with it that can be done."

HAL LINDSEY

I pray to God, but not every time there's a problem. It depends on what the problem is. Just praying may not resolve problems, but He will help you work it out or maybe give you guidance. But I don't think He is going to change things that much. However, He will help you to change things or understand them better.

GLEN CAMPBELL

One of my friends went off as a missionary in Thailand, and I do think that one of these days I might say, "Let's take a few years off and go on a mission." But I think it's more likely that I will continue combining show business with preaching and with teaching. That way I might be more effective than if I were preaching in one place.

PAT BOONE

I have felt all my life that the good Lord has had His arms around me . . . and I'm so grateful.

LAWRENCE WELK

Just before I went overseas, my dad sent me a copy of the 91st Psalm. "My dear Jim boy," his letter read, "I feel sure that God will lead you safely through this experience. I am staking my faith on that fact." Out of the envelope had dropped, almost unnoticed, a small booklet bearing the title, "The Secret Place — A Guide to the 91st Psalm." I picked it up and started to read it. From that day forward, the little booklet was always with me. Before every bombing raid over Europe, I read some of it, and with each reading the meaning deepened and strengthened for me. The words and meaning of the 91st Psalm have carried me through my life.

JAMES STEWART

I believe that God guides us — even though we don't always realize this. Human beings can be stubborn creatures. Seems to me that sometimes God has to shove us and shove us before we're willing to let Him have a hand at straightening things out. And we don't even have the decency to be grateful to Him when He does. There were times I thought I was being pushed around . . . when I was really being guided.

DORIS DAY

I praise and thank the Lord Jesus Christ for His gift of Everlasting Life, through the Cross of Calvary and His resurrection. I *know* my Redeemer lives, because I see Him living in the heart and life of America. In following Him, I too have experienced my Garden of Gethsemane and my Calvary — but it was glorious, because He was with me. He brought me safely through to the resurrection of a new life, filled with love, service, hope, and Christian peace, the peace that passes all understanding. Yes, I *know* in whom I have believed!

DALE EVANS ROGERS

I just figure that the good Lord is taking care of everything in His own way.

GLEN CAMPBELL

There's no death, I'm sure — only a physical separation. And when you've been really close to someone, you have a rapport that transcends the physical loss. Jesus did say there are dead people, though. And there are all those who won't love, feel, or respond to care.

DORIS DAY

The Bible tells us very plainly that "God was *in* Christ," right there on the Cross "reconciling the world (us) to Himself!" We were so far out of line that God knew *nothing* short of showing us what the inside of His Great Heart really looked like could change us! And to see inside a heart, we must see blood! On the Cross, God let His Own Heart break in that tremendous moment when He *took* our sinful natures into His Own Heart and smothered them to death! It broke His Heart, but it also breaks the power of sin in our lives — *when* we make an eternal agreement through Christ with the God who loved us enough to die for us! Enough to take *our* sin into His Own Heart. Enough to take our place on the Cross and let us go free.

EUGENIA PRICE

I've been a religious man all my life. Down in Tennessee my father was an elder and a deacon in the church. The elders asked me to leave that church. They believe in miracles only in the first century to prove the tenets of Christianity, and that God acts now only through natural law and providence. But I believe differently; I believe that God still performs miracles in our world.

PAT BOONE

A man of any race, a man of any nationality, a man of any language can believe, and that's all God says you have to do to get to heaven — just believe. Now that word "believe" may be a little more than you think it is. It means commitment; it means surrender; it means that I give everything that I have to Jesus Christ and trust Him alone for my forgiveness and my salvation.

REV. BILLY GRAHAM

As for witnessing — this is an old battle. Bob knows how difficult this always has been for me. It's a case of having to strip away your ego completely, to lay your soul bare for the Lord. There may be only a little time left in which we can speak up for Jesus, yet I feel a lack within myself. I feel so inadequate and limited, partly, I realize, because I really don't know the Bible sufficiently well. Yet Bob continues to exhort me to share my Christian testimony, no matter how difficult this may be for me. And my heart also tells me I must share Jesus, even when my courage fails me. So audiences know from the outset that I'm a Baptist. And at the end of the act, when I speak of Christ and sing what I've come to think of as our witness songs, I believe the Holy Spirit takes over and helps us communicate something our show never before could get across.

ANITA BRYANT

I know some people claim to be atheists, but you have to believe in something. However, I don't think you have to go to church to worship or prove you're religious.

GLEN CAMPBELL

I believe that the youth of this country have not lost religion; they are just disillusioned with the lack of it and evidences of bigotry and hypocrisy in the very houses of worship they attend, or have stopped attending.

PAT BOONE

I believe in God as my Creator and His Son as my Saviour. They have been my constant companions for a long time. And even at the point of death they will not leave me.

JAMES STEWART

I went to every church when I was a kid — even the Holy
Roller church, because I dug its singing. I'm very broad-
minded about religion. There's one God, so why all these
denominations going in different directions?

GLEN CAMPBELL

In the Communist world, everyone serves the state. In our
world, we serve God and each other. A hundred years ago,
Abraham Lincoln was sworn in as President. He said,
"Intelligence, patriotism . . . and a firm reliance on Him who
has never yet forsaken this favored land, are still competent
to adjust in the best way our present difficulty." Those
words still hold, like an embedded anchor.

PAT BOONE

The great truth that Jesus wants us to know is that He chose
to live his life as He expects us to live, in a moment-by-
moment reliance upon the Father who worked through Him
by the Holy Spirit. That fantastic life that the world knew
as the life of Jesus was actually lived not *by* Jesus but *in* Him
by the Holy Spirit.

HAL LINDSEY

Many years ago, I joined a little band in Texas and all of
those boys were drinking heavily, and some of them were
smoking weed. I didn't stay there too long. It went too much
against my grain. But I can tell you that not many of them
have lasted; I think it's sad, because you just can't go against
the wisdom that's been handed down through the ages. My
upbringing is Christian, and I try to live with the laws Christ
gave us, which has worked out very well for me.

LAWRENCE WELK

When we speak of Christian faith, we refer to certain beliefs and doctrines. These are of great importance, for Christian living presupposes Christian conviction. But it is possible to have beliefs which do not find expression in conduct. This belief of the head is often confused with real faith. The simple truth is: one really believes only that which he acts upon.

REV. BILLY GRAHAM

There are three things in a man's life; loneliness, a certain kind of woman, and God.

JOHNNY CASH

I think the happiest people in the world are those who live Christmas every day of their lives, just as they do their religion. With faith in God, obstacles are only a challenge you can meet.

LAWRENCE WELK

Someone has described the Bible as "man's attempt to find God." I think it may also be a record of God's attempt to find man and guide him, but let's not argue over that. It is enough for us to know that the Bible holds the Word and the words of God spoken to men from Adam in Eden to John on Patmos. The Bible is God's Word, not man's. It is God calling to us as we walk the earthly way, telling us which way to turn, how to avoid the stumbling blocks and the thieves who lie in wait . . .

DALE EVANS ROGERS

Religion is my foundation.

PAT BOONE

The plain fact is people are indifferent to an academic and
pedantic pulpit, but they will come back and throng about a
pulpit that is spiritually vital, spiritually powerful and
spiritually challenging and interesting. Put the Cross at the
center, summon to personal sacrifice, hold up high standards,
make stern demands; in other words give real Christianity to
the people and the men will be separated from the boys.

DR. NORMAN VINCENT PEALE

God stands before us in Jesus Christ offering every grace,
every power, every healing, every strength, every joy we
need. "For it pleased the Father that in him should all fullness
dwell." The all-encompassing need of every human being
has already been met in Christ. He is there, available, waiting
— even moving toward us, prodding us to receive. "Come
unto me, all ye that labour and are heavy laden, and I will
give you rest." Jesus Christ is not a religious theory
concocted by the mind of man. He is the living God and He
is there with you now, waiting for you to receive. Waiting
for me to receive. Waiting for us to grasp the difficult
simplicity of acceptance from His hands.

MARJORIE HOLMES

I've been to all kinds of churches, including synagogues,
because I want to know the difference between the various
faiths.

GLEN CAMPBELL

Your lips must become the lips of the resurrected Christ, to
speak His messages, to be His witness. This means that the
harsh, unkind words remain unspoken.

REV. BILLY GRAHAM

A church that disregards its function as a free and open house
of God for all people of whatever economic status, national
origin or color is not a true church of the Lord Jesus Christ.
Any church which crassly and deliberately repels any of
God's children deserves to lose its tax exemption under law
since this financial relief by the government is related to the
true churchly function of serving all people at all times —
and we mean *all* people.

DR. NORMAN VINCENT PEALE

As I walk His way with this satisfied singing soul, all around
me seems to be singing too. It is a blessed, happy walk, and I
enjoy it as a sheep would enjoy being turned loose in a good
green pasture to enjoy food and rest. I came to Him and He
gave me rest.

DALE EVANS ROGERS

My faith is far from perfect. I admit there have been times
in my life when, through lack of faith, I felt God had failed
me. I would pray for a sin of mine, wanting Him to take it
from me, yet not willing within myself to give it up. God,
knowing me so well, allowed me to feel the pain of this even
as I impatiently turned my back on Him. Also there have
been times in my life when I was just not myself — times
when I wondered if there were even a shred of godliness left
in me. I was tempted, and struggling for my soul. I really
thought I was going to lose it. At one time I was having such
difficulties in my marriage and in other human relationships,
and got so weary of my own sinfulness, that I felt strongly
tempted to sever with God. Yet something made me hang on.
I know that must have been God with me.

ANITA BRYANT

MONEY

Pat Boone *Anita Bryant* *James Stewart*
Billy Graham *Johnny Cash* *Norman Vincent Peale*
Glen Campbell *Marjorie Holmes* *Lawrence Welk*
Doris Day *Eugenia Price* *Hal Lindsey*
Dale Evans Rogers

Think of the things that cannot be bought with money. It
cannot buy health, friends, love, or peace of mind and heart.
It cannot buy peace of soul. We come to the conclusion then,
that money in itself is not worthy of the importance most
people place upon it.

REV. BILLY GRAHAM

Oh, God, give me more faith in your abundance. Help me
to stop worrying about money so much. Let me spend less
time fretting about material things. I often envy other people
their possessions. Forgive me. I sometimes feel an actual pain
in the presence of people whose dress and manner speak of
ease and wealth. Forgive me this very real sin. I do not covet
— no, for I don't wish them less. Only I am anxious for more,
so much more. And this is worry. It is putting emphasis upon
the wrong things. It bespeaks my lack of faith. Lord, help me
to remember how generously you have endowed the earth.
That you have lavished upon us more food than any of us
can consume. More clothing than any of us can wear. More
treasures than we can carry. And that it is your will that each
of us have his portion. A fine full portion to meet all our
needs. Help me to realize what my real needs are. And to be
thankful. For so long as I trust in you all these needs are
being, and will be met. (You said it is hard for a rich man to
enter the kingdom of heaven. Perhaps it's even harder for a
poor man who wants to be rich!)

MARJORIE HOLMES

We never had no money when I was a boy, but I was never hungry either. Aw, sometimes at supper we had to fill up on turnip greens and sometimes at breakfast it was just fatback and biscuits — but that was plenty.

JOHNNY CASH

There's nothing wrong with being rich. Some of the greatest men of the Bible were rich. But it's what we do with our riches that God is going to look at, and our motives, and our intent.

REV. BILLY GRAHAM

It has been my good fortune to have a well-planned series of investments. I will never be hungry. I will always be able to get more or less whatever I want. But money is not an obsession as far as I am concerned. It *can* be a curse but it can also be a blessing if it is used to help others — this I have always tried to do. If I did less, it would be displeasing to my God. He allows us to earn a certain amount of money from time to time but He expects us to use that money wisely, and in His service and to His glory whenever and wherever possible.

DORIS DAY

Yes, I have money, other material blessings. But I have them with peace of mind because what God has enabled me to earn has been earned honestly, not by betraying or robbing others. People who constantly cheat and steal often may not be punished in this life but once they meet God in the next life, they will see how foolish it was to ever imagine that they could get away with it all.

LAWRENCE WELK

We should keep the record and the principles straight here.
Jesus never said that money was evil *in itself*. What He said
was that our misdirected *love* of money was the *root* of all
evil. I think Jesus believed in free enterprise; His parable of
the talents indicates that to me. I believe He expected us to
use our God-given talents to make as good a living as we
can, to acquire and use our possessions well, *but never to make
possessions the great goal in life.*

DALE EVANS ROGERS

How many of you are well-to-do? You have a good job, you
have an automobile, you have a television set, you have a nice
home to go to, you have three square meals a day, you're
pretty rich. You have a certain amount of security, but if
these are more important than Christ, you have the worst
kind of poverty — spiritual poverty. You're very, very,
very poor. You have no riches toward God.

REV. BILLY GRAHAM

I've taught our children that having money is no excuse for
not doing a fair share of work. All the children had regular
chores around the house and they were expected to do them
without question.

LAWRENCE WELK

They say I make more than a million dollars a year. Billie
doesn't like to talk about money and neither do I. But
sometimes — and I'm as serious as I can be — you really
can't tell the difference between the rich times and the poor.
It has something to do with growing up with a family full of
love and music and understanding.

GLEN CAMPBELL

Nobody was poorer than me. I used to get on the farm 10
cents a year for spending money — ten cents a year. But now
through opportunity and work this world has become heaven
on earth for me.

LAWRENCE WELK

Dear God, surely it's not the love of money that is the root
of all evil, at least in marriage . . . it is in not knowing how to
divide it wisely. How much am I free to spend, without
feeling guilty? How much is my husband, without my
resenting it? When I earn money is it mine to do with what I
want? Or am I obliged to turn it over to him and then ask for
some of it back? I am all confused about this, Lord, I am
upset. And my husband is, too. But when we try to talk it
over and come to some conclusions, either we hurt each
other by being too frank, or we hold back and harbor the
hurt of things left unsaid. And there is too much worry about
money in our marriage, Lord. The needs of a home and
family never shrink and they never stop, they only multiply
and swell. They are crowding out fun and affection, they
cast their shadow over the whole relationship. It is as if we
were separated by a vast pile of paper — bills and mortgages
and tax forms; or as if we were cut off from each other by a
wall of material demands — the car, the house, the things the
children need. Dear Lord, restore to us some perspective.
Guide us back to the essentials. Help me to realize that
companionship is more important than even physical
comforts; that material security means nothing if there isn't
emotional security as well. Dear God, please help us to
resolve our misunderstandings. Give us either more money
or more sense.

MARJORIE HOLMES

John D. Rockefeller made his millions in oil, but if a benevolent God had not put the oil in the ground, and hadn't endowed man with the sense to refine and market it, there would be no fortunes in oil.

REV. BILLY GRAHAM

Work and money are the freedom twins. Money in the bank means greater freedom of mind and action and we don't get financial security without working hard for it.

PAT BOONE

We were real poor when I was growing up, but I never knew it — it was that kind of family. But we had an old rickey house in the bottom country near an old slough. We had an old pot-bellied stove. For baths we'd run down to the creek or jump in the family washtub on Saturday night. I cut wood, slopped the hogs, milked the cows, picked cotton, gathered corn. I had to plow, hoe, get the horses in, get the cows in. If Daddy said something, it was "Yes sir," with no back talk and no sass.

GLEN CAMPBELL

I got this idea of singin' for a livin' because I was starvin' to death. So I went up to the office of Sun Records and tried to get someone to listen to me. It wasn't easy. I didn't say much but I came back often. I had to sit there and stare for a long time.

JOHNNY CASH

Fern and I had tremendous financial hardships when we were first married. Those hardships have made us a lot closer.

LAWRENCE WELK

I finally worked up the courage to ask my father to lend me the four hundred dollars I needed for an accordion. I promised him that I would stay on the farm for four years — until I was twenty-one — and I would turn over all the money I earned from playing in bands to the household. He agreed after much thought. To this day, I don't know what motivated him. True, he had struck a very good bargain. On the other hand, he put himself in debt to the tune of four hundred dollars, at a time when most farmers earned less in a full year's work, and this represented a staggering amount of confidence and trust in one of his eight children. Perhaps he understood me and my dreams better than I thought.

LAWRENCE WELK

Money is a gift of God, and it is to be used for His glory. If it is squandered selfishly, or employed greedily, it cankers and brings misery and distress upon him who possesses it.

REV. BILLY GRAHAM

You were born into a world in which "money talks" and in which "a man must have money to live," according to those who claim to know the ways of the world. You must eat and you must have clothes to cover your nakedness and you need a house to live in. There's no denying that. A lot of people will tell you that this all counts up to just one thing — you'd better make money, the more the better insofar as security is concerned, and make it as fast as you can, for if you don't take care of yourself nobody else will ... It isn't enough just to get money; anything goes, no holds are barred, no bothersome morality or religion should stand in the way of your getting it.

DALE EVANS ROGERS

Although we always taught our kids the value of money, we never had them on allowances. I don't see any reason to treat your children like salesmen on an expense account.

JAMES STEWART

The making of money is necessary for daily living, but money-making is apt to degenerate into money-loving, and then the deceitfulness of riches enters in and spoils our spiritual life.

REV. BILLY GRAHAM

I'm now in the world of the silver-gray limousine. They're at the airfields when I arrive. In the old days, we'd go downtown and walk around and go to the movies and stores. We don't do that anymore. A security guard sits outside my room all night. People ask me for favors. They've put all this power into my hands. I'm kind of astounded by it, and I'm scared to death because of the influence my name and words might have.

JOHNNY CASH

I think it's important, no matter how rich you become, to always remain able to live a normal life, without any money at all. It's dangerous to step up your standard of living so much, and be so dependent upon it, that you couldn't cope if misfortune came your way.

JAMES STEWART

Tell me what you think about money, and I can tell you what you think about God, for these two are closely related. A man's heart is closer to his wallet than almost anything else.

REV. BILLY GRAHAM

CRISIS

Pat Boone Anita Bryant James Stewart
Billy Graham Johnny Cash Norman Vincent Peale
Glen Campbell Marjorie Holmes Lawrence Welk
Doris Day Eugenia Price Hal Lindsey
Dale Evans Rogers

We must *face* evil, not run from it; because when we run, evil pursues. Evil must be "stared down." Thousands are neurotics today because they try to escape problems, only to face bigger ones farther down the line. This is something we need to teach our children early. Many children start such neuroses by lying to avoid unpleasant issues, and the habit becomes a malignant one.

DALE EVANS ROGERS

I've felt the power of God. I called for help and I got it. What happened wasn't dramatic, but to me it was a miracle. I got a tooth infection in Canada one year and went to a dentist who pulled the wrong tooth. At first, of course, I thought it was going to be all right, but it wasn't. I was in such pain — oh, such pain! At three o'clock in the morning, I was literally crying because my tooth hurt so much. I began to pray and my tooth quit hurting, and I went to sleep. The Good Lord took care of me.

GLEN CAMPBELL

Just before I got off pills, I was in a cloud all the day. I saw everything as though it was in a haze. I saw people as though they were ghosts floating in a mist. I didn't know what was happening. I didn't even know, half the time, if I was sitting or standing. And I couldn't remember today where I had been yesterday. Death had its arms around me. Another week and I would have been dead at 33.

JOHNNY CASH

It is hard to be a Christian . . . but glorious; and it is the most exciting venture of life — because Christ *is* life! You know the saying about airplane pilots reaching the "point of no return" on a trip? I have passed the point of no return on my Christian pilgrimage. I am sure the way henceforth will be steep and perilous, but my Guide is dependable and He promises the summit, even though we may be gasping when we reach there. Jesus is the Pearl of Great Price, and in order to possess Him eternally, it may be necessary to forfeit dearly. But let me ask you, what else is there? St. Paul says, "Having done all, stand!" Lord, help me to stand straight and unflinching (in crisis). You have given and suffered so much for us. Why should we expect a rosy and smooth path?

DALE EVANS ROGERS

Troubles have a way of assuming undue proportions, and even a small difficulty can so magnify itself that the entire landscape is dominated by it. He is, you might say, a pompous tough guy, vaunting himself like a little man with an inferiority complex, who finds his defense in assuming larger proportions than he merits. Usually the person who worries reflects so constantly upon his troubles, those he has and those he expects, that his whole sky seems dark and gloomy. Now let him begin to affirm and dwell upon the good things in his life and he will find them better company. They are more modest and do not intrude themselves nor become assertive until they are made by continued association to feel at home. But when that time comes, how they seem to increase in numbers and their glad voices make the dreary old house of a man's mind a cheery place once more! Herein lies the secret of effectiveness in living.

DR. NORMAN VINCENT PEALE

For many, this entering into the Spirit-filled life is a crisis experience. If for years you've been wallowing in defeat in your Christian life and suddenly the indwelling Christ becomes magnificently alive to you, you may feel like you've been zapped!

HAL LINDSEY

Life's tragedies and hardships and heartbreaks, whether they come from death or illness or accident or broken friendships, can either make us or break us! All around us we see people who have been broken by their sorrow. But, just as surely, the hard knocks can *make* us! They can push us forward, if we let them! *If* we are willing to follow the example of the Lord we claim to follow.

EUGENIA PRICE

How much are we supposed to stand, God? How much can the human spirit bear? Trial is piled upon trial. And before one crisis is survived another bears down. I am buffeted and bruised; I am knocked almost witless, yet I know I must keep my wits about me. I must keep my senses and remain strong, I must proceed. It is as if these crises bear human faces and they encompass me like enemies, knocking me this way and that between them, crying for my help even as they beat me well nigh unconscious. God, help me to remember that life is full of tribulation. And though you do not always deem it right or wise to help me, yet you *are* helping simply by being there. My strength comes from you. Thank you. My courage comes from you. Thank you. Deep, deep within me, implanted by your very hands, is my determination, my toughness, my will to survive.

MARJORIE HOLMES

When I was a little girl, I wanted to be a dancer. That was
to be my dream; my career. I built all my hopes around that.
Then, when I was 15, my leg was injured in an automobile
accident. I lived in a plaster cast for long months. It was
thought that I would never walk again. During my forced
inactivity, I began to develop my singing voice. I took lessons
and studied hard. And this was the turning point in my life.
For it was the beginning of my career and my success as a
singer. Now I know the real meaning of the words 'Every
cloud has a silver lining.' It's only another way of saying that
all things work together for good.

DORIS DAY

If you are in sorrow as you read this, please don't think I'm
trying to belittle your grief or tell you it isn't important. It is
important. It is so important to the Lord Jesus that He is
sharing it with you right now! And He is saying to you,
"*You and I* can take this thing and shine it up and find a way
to use it so that you, My child, will grow up in spiritual
maturity and depth of character. Then, you will be able to
help other people whose lives are also struck with sorrow."
Jesus is asking us all if we are *willing* to follow Him and trust
Him to heal us even when everything seems black and there
seems to be no way out of our trouble?

EUGENIA PRICE

When we stop trusting the Holy Spirit to deliver us from
temptations and seek to handle them ourselves, we are
guaranteeing a spiritual nose dive. The inevitable result of
the activity of the flesh is sin, and sin will short-circuit the
power of God in the life of a believer.

HAL LINDSEY

My God is a God of strength and wisdom. He knows how to sustain me through every crisis. And He has never once failed. I have trusted Him with my life and He has taken care of me day after day.

PAT BOONE

In the years to come I just hope that my health will hold up so I can continue to be active . . . because I love my work. And I feel the worst is all behind me and the best ahead. I've had my share of difficult times but I'm not complaining. Troubles should purify a person and teach him not to make the same mistake twice.

LAWRENCE WELK

When Marty Melcher — my friend, my husband and my producer — died, there was such a void in my life that nothing seemed to matter any more. I cared about nothing. Finally, after several months, my son Terry told me that it was time for me to go back to work. I told him that I had no intention of going back to work — that I'd sit in the backyard and stare at flowers, or bake in the sun in Palm Springs. Very gently, Terry reminded me that for my whole life I had done things according to principle, but now I was not thinking of principle, only of myself. Terry said that if I went back to work I would be fulfilling my obligation to my contract, and I would come to peace with myself.   And, deep as my void was, I knew then that I could get the strength to do what Terry recommended if I were to go to my Source. As everybody can, I had only to ask for it, as everybody does. So, as I always do when I feel insecure and uncertain, I said, 'God, guide me.' He's never failed to help me.

DORIS DAY

I'll never forget the ragin', screamin' terrors I suffered when
I got off the pills. I dreamed the most horrible things. I'd
dream my stomach was popping full of big glass balls. And
they'd start pulling me, and they'd pull so hard I'd be flying.
They'd lift me clear up into the stars, and finally they'd break
into thousands of splinters all over my body. I'd see the
splinters in my arms and legs and then all of a sudden these
splinters would come to life and start wiggling. I'd wake up
in a horrible sweat, and it would only be about two minutes
later.

JOHNNY CASH

I would be less than honest if I were to pretend that Sandy's
death did not shake me, and that the manner of his passing
was not hard. But if you wonder whether I have come to the
place where I think that all this long struggle of Sandy toward
a goal he never reached — that it has all ended in bitter
disillusionment and defeat, or if you think that my faith has
been broken or destroyed by his mistaken acceptance of an
unworthy challenge in Germany, let me repeat to you the
words of St. Paul to the Romans: "For I am persuaded, that
neither death, nor life, nor angels, nor principalities, nor
powers, nor things present, nor things to come, nor height,
nor depth, nor any other creature, shall be able to separate
us from the love of God, which is in Christ Jesus our Lord."
Nothing could separate me, or Sandy, from that.
Nor do I fear for my own future, after all the tragedy that has
struck our home. The clouds of sorrow have been thick and
heavy, but they have always cleared away. I have reached the
point of no return, in my Christian experience, and with Job
I can cry, "Though he slay me, yet will I trust in him."

DALE EVANS ROGERS

I have met too many people who are virtually on the brink of mental illness because they think they have lost their salvation — that eternal life is no longer theirs. They believe they have committed some terrible sin, and the enemy comes in and says, "You have committed the unpardonable sin." Or, "You've committed some sin that God won't forgive you for at this time.". . . The helmet of salvation is knowing that your salvation is absolutely secure and complete. Once you believe in Jesus Christ you are forgiven for your sins — past, present, and future. Once you have believed in Him you can never be taken out of His family. Salvation does not depend upon performance. (NOTE: It does not vanish in some spiritual crisis.) It never has and never will. If you do not have that helmet or assurance of salvation, you cannot have a vitally strong faith.

HAL LINDSEY

Maybe you've come to a place in your . . . life when you think, "I've had it. So much is stacked against me; I can't run my life the way it ought to go. I'm worn out. I give up." Believe me, that's a great place to get . . . When you hit bottom spiritually, there's no place to go but up. God lets us exhaust every trick we have . . . When we're finally hanging on the ropes, He steps in and says, "Will you throw in the towel now and let Me take over?"

HAL LINDSEY

I know what it is to face a crisis. I have been in the midst of many of these in my life. The only answer is to look upward, not to self or other human beings. No crisis is so serious that it becomes unmanageable to God.

LAWRENCE WELK

During my bombing missions in the midst of World War II, God was with me every step of the way. I prayed to Him for guidance and He was there without ever once deserting me. If all of us could be as faithful to Him as He is to us, this world would be better off.

JAMES STEWART

A month later our beloved little Debbie was killed in a bus accident. Roy was in the hospital in a serious condition, following a spinal operation, and I was left to face it with the other children. The children were marvelous. Both Sandy and Dusty felt my pain; it got into their hearts, and there was a silent, sacred, spiritual, comforting bond between us without which I think I would have collapsed.

DALE EVANS ROGERS

Satan uses worry, anxiety and tension to really keep us off-balance. The gospel of peace is concerned with meeting worry with the promises of God. Are you afraid? Then claim this promise: "Do not fear, for I am with you; Do not anxiously look about you, for I am your God. I will strengthen you, surely I will help you, surely, I will uphold you with My righteous right hand." (Isaiah 41:10) Are you worried about your needs? Bills stacking up? Pressures of business closing in? Children or parents presenting problems which seem impossible to handle? Look at these promises and claim them: "Be anxious for nothing, but in everything by prayer and supplication with thanksgiving let your requests be made known unto God. And the peace of God which surpasses all comprehension, shall guard your hearts and your minds in Christ Jesus." (Philippians 4:6-7)

HAL LINDSEY

When I was a boy, my appendix ruptured, and before they could get me to a hospital, peritonitis had set in. In those days there were no miracle drugs to cure peritonitis; all the doctors could prescribe was rest, good care and prayer. I got all three. But for weeks I hovered between partial consciousness and deep coma-like sleep, with a tube in my side to drain off the poison. And then one day I had a dream so vivid that even today I remember it. I had on some sort of winglike apparatus, and I was flying. It was a wonderful sensation, and I had the feeling that if I would try just a little harder, I could fly right over the top of the sky and everything would be fine. I came to for a few minutes then. I had been spared, and the dream was the passing of my crisis. What a miracle it was! In later years when I thought about it, it seemed to me that God had given me a second chance at life, and I prayed for guidance to use my life in ways that would please Him most.

LAWRENCE WELK

If you are not strengthening the inner man by daily walking with God now, when a crisis comes you will quake with fear and give in, having no strength to stand up for Christ.

REV. BILLY GRAHAM

I been in jail twice, both times overnight. Both times it was for pills, dexedrine. Second time I woke up in a Georgia jail not knowing how I got there. Could've ended up on a chain gang, but the jailer was a fan of mine and he let it go. I was real hung up on those pills. I put my poor wife through hell with 'em. For years I was down to skin and bone, never sleeping, never eating. But that's all over now.

JOHNNY CASH

I say my tribulations had almost put me down. *Almost* — but let me add this: There have been many times in my life when I have beaten my fists against the walls in agony, but since I turned my life over to Jesus Christ, it has never once occurred to me to wail, "Christ, you've let me down." He has *never* let me down. He has always been there to grab my hand and lift me back on my feet again, to strengthen my feeble knees and still the tempests in my heart. Just when the rains and the winds of trouble seemed to have leveled my crop of dreams, I would catch the promise of a fresh root of blessing, and my faith was restored . . .

DALE EVANS ROGERS

My worries started when my doctor said very bluntly, "You'll either have to give up your work or your life." I had been feeling bad for some time, but I thought it was because I hadn't quite recovered from my gall bladder operation. But the doctor explained that I had a spastic colon — a condition that could not be cured, only treated. But I told my doctor that I couldn't accept what he said. I wasn't questioning the diagnosis; I was questioning the verdict. Dropping everything would have let too many people down. What I did do was curtail my activities — not stop them. My entire attitude toward life was altered from then on. I had always valued what I had, but suddenly each day became a gift to be thankful for.

LAWRENCE WELK

LOVE

Pat Boone Anita Bryant James Stewart
Billy Graham Johnny Cash Norman Vincent Peale
Glen Campbell Marjorie Holmes Lawrence Welk
Doris Day Eugenia Price Hal Lindsey
Dale Evans Rogers

I think love between a man and a woman can be beautiful.
But if it does not include a love for God and His Son, then it
will never be as wonderful as He would want it to be.

JOHNNY CASH

The greatest gift God gave married couples is *not* sex. It is
love. It's the totally honest, unselfish, in-depth love any
of us would give literally anything in this world to experience
. . .When two people build their home on Christian
principles, the highest kind of love can exist. The secret of
love is giving. Someone has said that sex begins at the
breakfast table, and I agree. It's a network of all the small
things a couple does, says and is together — the caring and
sharing, honesty and closeness, mistakes and forgiveness,
laughter, encouragement, obedience and trust. In I John
4:7-21, you'll find wonderful insights into what love is and
can be. Among other things, this passage advises, "Perfect
love casteth out fear." In a relationship that's merely physical,
fear can and almost surely will exist as one partner attempts
to hold the other through sexual attraction. The born-again
Christian, however, does not have to fear. His love is of God,
and therefore he can afford to trust. He can trust his partner,
because he first trusts the Son of God — Jesus! As Paul says
in 1 Corinthians 13:13, "And now abideth faith, hope and
charity, these three; but the greatest of these is charity
(love)." Love is God's greatest gift. All else follows.

ANITA BRYANT

The first time I fell in love I had chills up and down my spine. Fire sirens blowing. A party every night. I was sure that was love! It was an explosion! Then, when it didn't work out, I decided to be careful of those explosions!

DORIS DAY

I don't believe a man and a woman can really love each other outside of Christ. I believe that Christ gives a new depth — to married love. A new dimension of love. He can rekindle the love of your heart.

REV. BILLY GRAHAM

I love June better'n my first bicycle . . . or watermelon . . . or . . . I dunno . . . a new pair of shoes on a rocky road.

JOHNNY CASH

I have tried always to guide myself by all that is involved in love — love for my family, my fellow man but, most importantly, love for the God who created us. In return I have always felt secure in *His* love.

JAMES STEWART

Love is, or should be, their (offspring) birthright — even more than food and shelter and protection. They are entitled to it, and they need to be reminded that it is always there . . . Affection can be expressed in many ways, in a shared joke, a word, a glance, a touch. Small babies need to be cuddled and petted; if they are totally deprived of this, they become neurotic. We never fully outgrow this need for a gentle touch, although it is probably the first bond to disappear when things are going badly between people.

DR. NORMAN VINCENT PEALE

At times when I have felt lonely, the love of God comes to
me and gives me peace — the peace that passes all
understanding. It is a joyous moment, this communion with
Him.

JAMES STEWART

There is a sense in which true love is a fire. Genuine love can
never be complacent and passive. It is the man who loves his
school most who shouts the loudest for his team at a football
game.

REV. BILLY GRAHAM

Life is lonely alone. It's wonderful to work and achieve
success, but unless you have someone to share it with, it
doesn't mean much.

DORIS DAY

The more a man looks and searches, the more he realizes that
the only place he can find the compassion he needs is at home
among the people who love and understand him.

JOHNNY CASH

Fern and I give each other lots of elbow room, following our
separate hobbies. Sometimes, being together constantly can
have a bad reaction, even for people very much in love. The
lack of privacy can set off a spark of resentment. Separation
— in small doses — can bring people closer together. When
I'm away from Fern for a while, I can't wait to see her again.
I have an urge to tell her all the things that have happened to
me while I was away, and I'm anxious to know what's been
going on with her and the family.

LAWRENCE WELK

Above all, young people want a simple, personal and relevant answer to life that isn't based upon self-centered materialism, but upon real life, selfless love. When they are shown that this idealistic view of life cannot be achieved by various shades of welfarism, socialism, or drugs, but only through a personal relationship with Christ . . . then many respond and receive Jesus Christ.

HAL LINDSEY

I remember that two or three times I thought I was in love. They called it puppy love, but it was real to the puppy! I remember that one day I decided that I was going to wait on God. I didn't know that, way out in China, God was preparing a lovely young woman just for me. She was the right one in temperament and in her experience . . . God specially prepared Ruth to be my wife for this particular ministry that He called me to. God has chosen someone just for you. Wait on God. Get God's man, God's woman; and there will be little danger of a breakup of your marriage.

REV. BILLY GRAHAM

The Bible tells us in First John that actually *God is love*. He is the very source of love. Just as a river has a source, a place from which it springs first, so all love (if it is real love) springs from God Himself. His very Nature is love. And when God comes to dwell within us in the Person of the Holy Spirit, we have the very springs of love right there inside us! Are you beginning to see that we need not, we *cannot* cook up love toward God by our own efforts? He doesn't expect us to. He just says through Jesus Christ, "Come to Me" and I'll love you into loving Me!

EUGENIA PRICE

It seems that love is the real key to Christian unity. In the spirit of true humility, compassion, consideration and unselfishness, which reflect the mind of the Lord Jesus, we are to approach our problems, our work and even our differences.

REV. BILLY GRAHAM

When I became an adult, I realized that we are all vulnerable human beings, and whenever we put our love and faith into another human being, we are open to hurts and disappointments. That's just part of life. We all hurt each other, completely unintentionally at times. The only one to trust completely is God, and once you can understand that, and learn not to bear any malice or bitterness in your heart, your life will be much happier. I realized that the thing to do is live life as well as you can. Everything else is secondary.

LAWRENCE WELK

Oh, Lord, I don't feel loved anymore; I don't feel wanted. My children are so thoughtless. They demand so much of me and take it without appreciation. They overlook the things they could do for me, and when I ask their help they cruelly rebel. My husband is too preoccupied with problems even to suspect this awful vacancy I feel. I scarcely know my neighbors; and my friends are too busy with their own concerns to really care. Who would care, Lord, if I disappeared tomorrow? Who would really care? I know I am needed, and for that reason alone I would be missed. But *wanted*, Lord, really wanted as a person, for myself. You, Lord, you alone know and love and care about me . . . In you alone I find my understanding and my reassurance.

MARJORIE HOLMES

In life you get what you put into it. And if you put a lot of love into it, a lot comes back to you.

LAWRENCE WELK

The love of God is perfectly revealed at the Cross. "For he so *loved* the world that he gave his only begotten son . . ." What greater love could there be than to go through the agony of Calvary in order to offer sinners salvation?

DALE EVANS ROGERS

Man is the expression of divine life, which neither begins nor ends. Our grief over the loss of a loved one is because we feel deprived, yet we really aren't. For no one can take love away from you but yourself, and the qualities we love in people are really spiritual attributes, and they cannot be restricted to a human personality.

DORIS DAY

God loves you. You're rebellious, you cheat, you commit immorality, you're selfish, you sin, but God loves you with an intensity beyond anything that I could describe to you. He loves you, and He loves you so much that He gave His only son Jesus Christ to die on that cross and the thing that kept Christ on that cross was love, not the nail.

REV. BILLY GRAHAM

Most women are smart, but still they like to be referred to as the weaker sex. That's okay, so long as they don't get carried away in a love relationship — as I was. It doesn't make a woman less of a woman if she knows what's going on in her man's world; after all, it's part of her world, too.

DORIS DAY

I know that they live again, my dear ones whom I no longer can see. You have not taken them into a kingdom — they wouldn't be happy in a kingdom — but you have opened wide for them a place of joy and peace . . . where their dreams can be fulfilled . . . They know how much I miss them, they know how much I love them. They understand about all the things I meant to do for them and didn't, all the words I failed to say. They put their arms around me to comfort me. They tell me, "It's all right, human love is faulty but for all its faults enduring. It goes beyond such things, it goes beyond even this separation. The loss of the body does not mean the loss of that love. There is a new life in which that love is even stronger. For God is love, remember God is truly love." And this I know. This, God, I know: They are with you now — forever. And so with me forever — in this new dimension of love.

MARJORIE HOLMES

To make a good man and keep him good you got to have a good woman.

JOHNNY CASH

The love of God is wonderful. If it is present in a marriage where love between husband and wife also exists, life is made truly meaningful. I've known God's love for a long time now, and I can tell you that my life would be emptier without it.

GLEN CAMPBELL

God's love is available to all of us through His Son, the Lord Jesus Christ. We just need to accept this fact, and His Holy Spirit will indwell us.

PAT BOONE

MARRIAGE

*Pat Boone Anita Bryant James Stewart
Billy Graham Johnny Cash Norman Vincent Peale
Glen Campbell Marjorie Holmes Lawrence Welk
Doris Day Eugenia Price Hal Lindsey
Dale Evans Rogers*

God's Word is our only authority. The Bible teaches us how to love and discipline a child, guides us as husband to wife, wife to husband, and as to correction, reproof, and instruction. Anything we need can be found in the Bible.

ANITA BRYANT

My home is the place I'd rather be than anywhere else in the world.

JAMES STEWART

Scripture is very clear as to what the attitude of the family should be one to another. "Except the Lord build the house, they labour in vain that build it." How true I have found that to be! I can honestly and humbly say to you that if Jesus Christ had not come into our lives some years ago, our marriage probably would not have survived. Shortly after giving my heart and life to Christ, someone sent me a little book titled, *In His Steps.* That book impressed and greatly benefited me spiritually. It was the story of a few consecrated Christians who made a pact to conduct their lives in every situation on the basis of "What would Jesus do?" It is a wonderful book and I wish every Christian would read it. Just think what one family could accomplish for the Lord, if each member would really try to do what he thought Jesus would have him to do! No telling how far their good influence would reach.

DALE EVANS ROGERS

We are finding that disrespect for each other before marriage cannot change to respect after marriage. Love is not lust, and lust is not love. Love, if it is anything at all, is respect; and when respect for the other's dignity and integrity is thrown aside, love folds up like a punctured balloon.

REV. BILLY GRAHAM

I am convinced that in normal people the requirements for a happy marriage — understanding, tolerance, kindness, unselfishness — almost always exist in adequate quantities. It's when these qualities become stifled or blocked by lack of maturity, lack of self-discipline, lack of control that trouble begins. That is when anger takes over, communication begins to fail, grievances begin to be magnified out of all proportion, happy memories are brushed aside and forgotten. And unless corrective steps are taken, the marriage can easily pass the point of no return on the toboggan slide toward divorce.

DR. NORMAN VINCENT PEALE

It seems as though I've been married all my life.

GLEN CAMPBELL

I think there has been too much emphasis placed on the possibility that differences between husband and wife in taste and temperament can cause marital difficulty. Why can't variety of outlook and contrast between natural individual reactions serve to enhance and vitalize a marriage, rather than endanger it? In many respects, Shirley and I are opposites. She is organized, efficient, purposeful. What a break for a guy who leans toward the disorganized, inefficient, easily-diverted style.

PAT BOONE

I feel that very often in marriage one partner will become terribly strong and take over, and I'm old-fashioned and believe that the man should run things. But of course that can leave one very weak . . . and there is a problem if the strong one passes away.

DORIS DAY

Although I generally advise against marrying too young, Shirley and I made the right decision when we married so early. It gave us a sense of well-being and security — we knew we'd never be alone. And there was our own home to come to. And then there are the joys of physical and emotional love being fulfilled.

PAT BOONE

Even in the worst of marriages, with the help of good counseling with a minister (and prayer, prayer, *prayer*) divorce can be avoided and a happy relationship established. I think it's all a matter of the Spirit in the heart. Jesus was quite definite about this. He said, "Moses because of the hardness of your hearts suffered you to put away your wives: but from the beginning it was not so." You see, divorce was *permitted*, but it was never God's purpose.

DALE EVANS ROGERS

These days many marriages fail because a lot of young people want to do their own thing. That doesn't work. It's just like a band. You can't have a group of musicians all doing their own thing. You have to be disciplined and work together. The same thing is true of marriage. When both sides are selfish, the marriage is in trouble.

LAWRENCE WELK

The family should be a closely knit group. The home should
be a self-contained shelter of security; a kind of school where
life's basic lessons are taught; a kind of church where God is
honored; a place where wholesome recreation and simple
pleasures are enjoyed.

REV. BILLY GRAHAM

A Christian home never comes about by accident. I believe it
must require more grace and hard work than any other
organization on earth.

ANITA BRYANT

Believe me, the marriage counselor or the minister who tries
to help shaky marriages is up against a tough job. Matrimony
is probably the most difficult as well as the most rewarding of
all relationships. It makes enormous demands on people, often
before they are mature enough to handle such demands. The
need for patience and tolerance and adjustment never ceases.
The daily requirements of sacrifice and selflessness never
grow less. No wonder, knowing the centrifugal forces within
any marriage, society used to chain two people together and
throw away the key!

DR. NORMAN VINCENT PEALE

You have to grow up to realize that there's no room in love
for games. There is room only for devotion. You know
you're in love when you think of someone else's happiness as
much or more than your own. It was a revelation to me,
something I didn't realize could happen. I always thought of
love as super excitement, but the man I married and loved for
seventeen years (Marty Melcher) was my *friend*.

DORIS DAY

Shirley and I loved the life here in Hollywood, but we moved for the sake of our girls. The kids are noticing that the children in their school are chauffered in Rolls Royces, and that practically a whole circus entertains for them at parties. We want some different values for our girls.

PAT BOONE

It's often been said that the family that prays together stays together. We think that's also true of the family that plays together.

JAMES STEWART

The idea that the family is the cornerstone of society is as old as the written word. Two thousand years ago, Cicero said, "The seat of empire is at the fireside." He meant that the home is the place where the ideals that keep civilization going are passed from one generation to another.

DR. NORMAN VINCENT PEALE

It is high time that our so-called experts on marriage, the family, and the home, turn to the Bible. We have read newspaper columns and listened to counselors on the radio; psychiatrists have had a land-office business. In it all, the One who performed the first marriage in the Garden of Eden and instituted the union between man and wife has been left out.

REV. BILLY GRAHAM

You have to become mature enough to realize God wants you to bring His spirit to your small children, your cantankerous old husband, and the everyday things of life. That's where it's hardest.

ANITA BRYANT

Raising children, I have discovered, is an almost insurmountable problem. No parents can completely solve it. They can only do what they think is best. Gloria and I never believed in rules and regimentation. In the Army there are regulations, it's all in the book. But there is no book on raising children. You have to treat each child according to his or her personality.

JAMES STEWART

Neither God, nor law, nor custom has ever decreed that we build our lives around our children. There are parents who, without meaning to do so, try to devour their children's time to the exclusion of their own plans. If only these parents could realize that their job is done once the child reaches adulthood.

LAWRENCE WELK

Families are drifting farther and farther apart in today's society. They aren't close. They don't share the way they used to. Shirley and I believe sharing religion makes a family closer. We have love to bind us, but in our home, it is our religion that holds us together.

PAT BOONE

The Supreme Court of the United States declared some time ago that "marriage is an institution, in the maintenance of which in its purity, the public is deeply interested, for it is the foundation of the family and of society, without which there would be neither civilization nor progress," and that "any trend or system which attacks the home condemns itself as hostile to public and personal welfare."

REV. BILLY GRAHAM

Billie and I have been married for 14 years and we run everything like a team — the house, the kids. Sure, we have our squabbles — any married couple who says they don't are liars. But if you're married to the right person, marriage is the greatest thing in the world.

GLEN CAMPBELL

Realism in marriage . . . calls for acceptance; in many areas you have to *accept* your married partner as they are, not as you'd like them to be. You must take them as they are, love them as they are.

DR. NORMAN VINCENT PEALE

The basic reason for unhappiness in the home is the fact that we have disregarded God and the principles He has given us. We have refused to acknowledge His plan for the family. The members of the home have refused to accept their particular responsibilities as given in the Bible.

REV. BILLY GRAHAM

Sometimes the husband and wife don't think alike about the necessity for God in their household, and this makes problems. But the biggest cop-out in the world is for the wife to blame a family's spiritual loss on the husband. I know because I've done it myself. It's a great excuse. You can pat yourself on the back to your girlfriends, saying, "Isn't it terrible? I want to go to church Sunday night, but he wants to watch television." That's a bunch of garbage. I knew I was lying when I said it. There's never been any time Bob didn't allow me to go to church, but there've been times when I used him as an excuse — when I didn't want to go.

ANITA BRYANT

An argument can be good for you — it blows off steam.
Before a couple marries, I strongly believe that they should
have an argument, even if they have to create one deliberately
to see how both will react.

LAWRENCE WELK

If you pray together, don't bore the children with long,
archaic prayers endlessly repeated. Make them short, intense
conversations with God. Pray about the problems that
children have, not just your own. Try to make them see that
prayer is not just an empty or meaningless recitation of things
that God knows already, but as Emerson said, "a way of
looking at things from the highest possible point of view."

DR. NORMAN VINCENT PEALE

Blessed is she whose daily tasks are a labor of love, for willing
hands and a happy heart translate into a privilege and her
labor becomes a service to God and to those she loves.
Blessed is she who opens the door to welcome both stranger
and well-loved friend, for gracious hospitality is a test of true
Christianity and spiritual stewardship. Blessed is she who
mends stockings and toys and broken hearts, for her
understanding is a balm to those in need. Blessed is she who
scours and scrubs. She knows that cleanliness is important,
but that forgiveness of sin in the human can only be purified
through the blood of Jesus Christ. Blessed is she who children
love, for the love of a child is more to be valued than fame
and fortune . . . Blessed is she who preserves the sanctity of
the Christian home, for hers is a sacred trust that crowns her
with dignity, and results in her children arising and calling
her blessed, and her husband praising her also.

DALE EVANS ROGERS

The Bible outlines very carefully the duties of husband, wife and children. The Bible warns that if you depart from these regulations concerning the family, you will be in serious difficulty and the happiness of your home will be in danger.

REV. BILLY GRAHAM

I teach my children the way I was taught. I was brought up with the idea of the father as head of the family. When he said something, you did it. It irks me to see a child sass a parent. If I had done that, I would have had my head knocked in.

GLEN CAMPBELL

I have the greatest respect for mothers and for the family. If we lose the family, we lose the whole country.

LAWRENCE WELK

Sometimes when a husband or a wife comes to me complaining bitterly about their marriage partner, I ask them to write down a list of all their mate's shortcomings. They usually perform this task with alacrity. Then I ask them to write — opposite each accusation — a quality that they once admired, or still admire in the other person. Sometimes they are able thus to balance the books, sometimes not. But I've never yet encounterd a case where the complainant was unable to find *something* good to say about the complainee! I then make them promise, within the next twenty-four hours, to say something complimentary about that particular characteristic to the owner of it. Very often this simple device proves to be a turning point in the whole relationship.

DR. NORMAN VINCENT PEALE

Duty is stern; love is winsome. The loving wife always has more fun in marriage because God planned it that way. He really does provide us with joy and abundant life if we'll just follow His blueprints. Christ becomes the means, then, toward perfecting and sanctifying a woman's cherished relationship to her man. In this way He fuses the two of them and creates a Christian marriage.

ANITA BRYANT

Living with Christian principles and God's way has a great deal to do with successful marriage. My wife and I have lived by the Golden Rule, the Ten Commandments and the Sermon on the Mount.

LAWRENCE WELK

Adults are less of a problem if they've done some hell raisin' when they were kids. But that doesn't mean that parents should let them do whatever they want without taking the consequences. I was strict with my kids, but fairly so. I was brought up by strict parents and feel that it is important that children are properly supervised. It builds character and self-control.

JAMES STEWART

At first Shirley didn't want me to kiss another woman in my movies. She felt that we both enjoyed our kisses together — and that maybe some other gal might too! But then she realized that she didn't have anything to worry about with me. And she came around to my way of thinking — that if a movie kiss is going to endanger a marriage, you don't have much of a marriage.

PAT BOONE

I'm not going to push my kids, they can do whatever they
want in life, these children. I just want them to be healthy
and treat other people well. I want them always to be
courteous and respectful to their elders.

GLEN CAMPBELL

As far as I'm concerned, children can be children. If that
means noise, confusion, occasional freshness or shouting or
bouncing, that is all right with me. But I do hope I know
where to draw the line. If you give youngsters rules to live
by, they'll find times when there are no given rules to cover
a situation. But if you give them principles (as my own
parents tried to do with me), they have a solid foundation on
which to build their lives.

PAT BOONE

Some call it life's greatest lottery. Marriage *can* be that, if we
are fools enough to think of it as a lottery or a gamble, or to
comfort ourselves with the thought, as some poor women do,
that "I can get a divorce and get out of it, if I don't like it."
If you want to smash your life to bits, that's a good
philosophy. But if you want to know one shining hour after
another, all your life long, try the Christian approach to
marriage.

DALE EVANS ROGERS

Mothers today need to take their responsibilities more
seriously than ever. Children are blessings from God, and it's
important to be with them, and oversee them every minute:
teaching, training, bringing them up in the admonition of the
Lord.

ANITA BRYANT

When Billie and I decided to get married, her father was upset. He didn't want his daughter to marry a musician. He believed musicians were fellows who ran around on their wives, but that wasn't the way Billie felt. She trusted me. We're very compatible. She would go hunting, fishing and water-skiing with me.

GLEN CAMPBELL

I pity parents who cling to their children and try to live their lives instead of enjoying things that are open to themselves alone. Lay away a tool and it gets rusty. Lay away your own hobbies, friends, activities, and you will kill your usefulness.

LAWRENCE WELK

One of our daughters told us that a schoolmate of hers had offered her marijuana and speed pills — right out of her purse. I asked my daughter her reaction. "I wasn't shocked," she told me, "I just don't need them." And I knew we'd done something right.

PAT BOONE

I look at my son and I think that maybe he is the only reason, that all my life has been nothing but a journey in time to reach these moments in time with my boy. All the hunger and bitterness and despair I have known before seem trivial now, just milestones on the way to completeness I have now. I wonder what I can do to help my boy grow straight and tall and sturdy, with his head held high and growing toward God, but his roots down strong and deep in this land. I keep looking and looking for ways to thank God for my family.

JOHNNY CASH

Over the years I've come to the conclusion that the easiest way to become a perfect husband is to make your wife believe you're listening to what she says, and then nod. I nod all the time, and I tell you, it works like a charm.

JAMES STEWART

Establish a daily family worship. Say a prayer of thanksgiving at each meal. Have a special time in the morning or evening when all the family gathers together to hear the Bible read and have prayer.

REV. BILLY GRAHAM

Everybody agrees that children should be given understanding, but I also believe in making them obey.

GLEN CAMPBELL

Most actors make terrible husbands — it's an occupational hazard. This is such a screwball business; you're always worrying about yourself in it. How do I look? How do I sound? There are so many pressures, so much competition, so much to think about, that most actors have little inclination to think about their wives and children.

JAMES STEWART

HAPPINESS

Pat Boone Anita Bryant James Stewart
Billy Graham Johnny Cash Norman Vincent Peale
Glen Campbell Marjorie Holmes Lawrence Welk
Doris Day Eugenia Price Hal Lindsey
Dale Evans Rogers

Many people are unhappy because they're victims of their
own envies and fears and hostilities. Just look at all the
discontented people you know. Unhappy, self-pitying, they
put a premium on the unattainable, wanting always something
that someone else has. Or they frighten themselves reading
in the paper about some new horror men have invented to
destroy one another; then they stop living today because
they're so terrified of tomorrow. These people are their own
victims, and they can change.

DORIS DAY

I could tell you of many people who have explored every
earthly source for happiness and failed, but eventually came
in repentance and faith to Christ and in Him found
satisfaction.

REV. BILLY GRAHAM

However ineffectual and unimportant and useless you may
feel, you are terribly important to God, and He needs you to
be your *best self* so that the part of His great plan which
concerns you, can be carried to its glorious completion. In
order to be your best self, you must begin now to understand
yourself, and He longs to help you on the way to true
happiness.

EUGENIA PRICE

Ah'm so happy I could bust. Ah'm having a ball.

JOHNNY CASH

People who follow the way of the world think they are happy. And for a while perhaps they are. But it is not a happiness that truly lasts. Only as saved ones in Christ can we know the true happiness offered by God.

HAL LINDSEY

You may search the world over for contented and happy men, but you will find them only where Christ has been personally and decisively received.

REV. BILLY GRAHAM

Sometimes, when the band plays so well I get goosebumps, or people come up to me at the end of our concerts and tell me how much our music has meant in their lives, I do feel almost sinful at the tremendous pleasure it all gives me. To be granted some kind of usable talent and to be able to use it to the fullest extent of which you are capable — this, to me, is a kind of joy which is almost unequaled. I have found it in music; my father in farming. I know others who have found it in practicing medicine, or running a bakery, or driving a truck — in running a bakery that makes the best kind of bread, or in driving a truck better than anyone else. That's the kind of achievement that makes a man happy.

LAWRENCE WELK

Being an actor means more to me than I usually let on. But let me tell you this story: Two people came up to me one day and said, "We don't know if this will mean anything to you, but we want you to know that we always enjoy your pictures." I told them, "Thank you. It means everything to me."

JAMES STEWART

We're to give thanks and praise to God in everything. This was the Apostle Paul's power, that he was able to count all as joy. My own special verse of Scripture — one I have claimed all my life — witnesses to Paul's Christian boldness: "I can do all things through Christ, which strengtheneth me."

ANITA BRYANT

We must always distinguish between wholesome, God-ordained pleasure and sinful, worldly pleasure. Christians have more wholesome fun than anyone in the world, but their joy wells up from within.

REV. BILLY GRAHAM

Have you ever found an electric train, or a bedraggled doll that belonged to you as a child and remembered how terribly important it was to you years ago? When we meet Christ face-to-face we're going to look back on this life and see that the things we thought were important here were like the discarded toys of our childhood. What a way to live! With optimism, with anticipation, with excitement. We should be living like persons who don't expect to be around much longer.

HAL LINDSEY

The flying bug hit me a long time ago, and just like the acting bug, it's something that's with you all your life. I still fly a one-engined Super Cub that's noisy and looks about 30 years old. But I can't get anybody to fly with me. Anyway, when you get up there in all that turbulence and know you're in control of a flying machine, it's great. It's very special. For me, it's therapy — total happiness.

JAMES STEWART

The joy of having children and experiencing their growth is the richest reward that life holds.

PAT BOONE

We weren't put here to have trouble and strife. Life should be wonderful — enjoying life is what it's all about. Be flexible; if you don't enjoy what you're doing, look for something else.

DORIS DAY

Happiness is being at peace; being with your loved ones; being comfortable and free of pain. But most of all, it's having those loved ones.

JOHNNY CASH

Christianity was never meant to be something to make people miserable, but rather something to make them happy.

REV. BILLY GRAHAM

Happiness is knowing my sins are forgiven, knowing that the penalty of those sins has been washed away by the Saviour's blood. Anything else is imperfect, for this forgiveness has never been equalled in its beauty and its ability to give peace and joy.

GLEN CAMPBELL

Real God-filled Christ-centered Christianity, with a man-sized depth emphasis on sin and a faith that is full of the tremendous joy of spiritual experience could give . . . a zest-packed life the like of which they (sinners) never knew existed.

DR. NORMAN VINCENT PEALE

Always look for new experiences, new friends, new viewpoints. That's part of growing and maturing. And that's what makes life a joy!

DORIS DAY

I'm happy to be alive — and lucky to be alive, and I finally know that I'm a good man.

JOHNNY CASH

And now as I dance I would offer up all the people I should be praying for. As I lift my arms in adoration I gather them in for your blessing. I see them happy. I see them well. This vision is vivid before me. As I dance I rejoice for their health, their happiness, their peace. These things I claim in your name for them. I dance for the people I love, oh, Lord. I dance their cares into your keeping. But I also dance for myself. For the joy and wonder of my own being. I dance in worship, to reach you.

MARJORIE HOLMES

I do the best I can every day. I don't worry about tomorrow until tomorrow. Instead, I just concentrate on what I'm doing at the minute — and have all the fun I can!

PAT BOONE

I can't talk very well, because talking doesn't happen to fit me. I have this accent, and I think that I must have been in this business for 20 years before I had the nerve to say 'ah-one and ah-two.' But I stuck with what I loved doing and I have been happy all my life. That's what our young people have to learn.

LAWRENCE WELK

There's a certain wonderful Christian freedom that comes from just being yourself. We've had comments that we have so much fellowship and fun at our parties, and some non-Christians comment they're amazed at how much fun they had, and there was no liquor, no carousing. They're surprised they could have such a good time in a Christian environment. If people could do more of this, it would help lead others to Christ.

ANITA BRYANT

My happiness is derived from knowing that the Holy Spirit is in control. I become unhappy only when I realize that *I* have re-assumed control. I get down on my knees and pray to God for the strength and the wisdom to put *Self* in the background, and let Him be constantly in the center.

PAT BOONE

Several times early in my career I debated about whether to return to the farm and forget my dreams. Maybe I would never make it. Well, as you can see, I didn't give up, and I'm so happy about it. I've been very fortunate to have had a lot of wonderful people come into my life as a result. Between my family and my work I have the most perfect life any man would want. I only wish that same happiness for every person.

LAWRENCE WELK

The greatest joy of my success was to be able to help other people — especially my folks. I retired Mom and Dad, bought them a house, bought them a car, and now they can do whatever they want to for the rest of their lives.

GLEN CAMPBELL

True happiness is from within, and does not depend on outward circumstances. When our sense of well-being depends on the things around us, we are in bad straits.

REV. BILLY GRAHAM

I am a very happy man. I sleep regular at night. I am a man that loves my work extremely. I have three families; my own, my musical family, and the family of listeners who follow my champagne music extremely.

LAWRENCE WELK

Happiness is being in the center of God's Will, knowing that you are acting as He wants you to do so. The most unhappy people are those who try to rebel against the Lord, going their own way without a thought as to whether their actions are honoring to Him or not. The person who is yielded to the control of the Holy Spirit can go through life with a wonderful confidence, a lack of fear of the future. The Lord who created everything is in charge.

DALE EVANS ROGERS

Happiness comes from within — you can't go out and buy it.

DORIS DAY

One important way for a Christian to witness is through having fun and being fun. Non-Christians sometimes think of us as stick-in-the-mud types. I think it's important for others to see Christ in you — and also to see that Christians can and do have a good time.

ANITA BRYANT

SUCCESS

Pat Boone Anita Bryant James Stewart
Billy Graham Johnny Cash Norman Vincent Peale
Glen Campbell Marjorie Holmes Lawrence Welk
Doris Day Eugenia Price Hal Lindsey
Dale Evans Rogers

With God's help, a man is capable of more success in what he is doing than he often believes. We under-rate our capabilities far too often.

DR. NORMAN VINCENT PEALE

As long as one competes *toward a goal* with a constructive attitude, the competitive effort is creative. It is when the competitive spirit so takes over that we become personally involved and emotionally offbase, that chaos follows. *Competition* nibbles at the basic peace of God's people like an energetic band of termites, and still most of us fail to recognize it for what it is. And on it goes unhampered, wrecking relationships and dreams.

EUGENIA PRICE

True success, lasting success comes as we pray to God for His Will to be manifested in our lives, for His purpose to guide us every step of the way. If we allow ourselves to become His instruments, there can be no real failure — only the greatest success of all, great because it is founded on our Lord and Saviour. The pursuit of success merely to earn us material blessings is sinful; for success then becomes an idol before which we fall in worship. Only as we try to glorify God in what we say or do can success become what He intended.

REV. BILLY GRAHAM

I expect audiences will get tired of me eventually. The only reason I've lasted this long is that I've had the sympathy of the audience all these years. In the parts I play the viewers feel a concern for me; they're not sure I'll win out, and they root for me.

JAMES STEWART

On some days the rest of my life stretches before me with such promise, Lord, such shining promise. Nothing is impossible, I can do anything I really want to do. I can be successful. I can be rich and famous if I want. I can love and marry a terrific man. But, above all, I can make some gift to this world you have let me enter. I must be here for some purpose, and that purpose will be revealed to me. Anyway, I *must* do something for it, if only to repay you for letting me be born in the first place. It's glorious to be alive, Lord. Thank you for creating me.

MARJORIE HOLMES

If all this fame went tomorrow, I wouldn't feel frustrated. I would go back to recording dates and producing records and writing songs. I used to accompany other people on my guitar. I could go back to that if my current success vanished. It wouldn't throw me.

GLEN CAMPBELL

Shirley and I were house-hunting in California. We heard about one place that went for $125,000. Shirley went to look at it, and when they found out who she was, it jumped to $140,000. Then I went to look at it with her, and it went up to $160,000.

PAT BOONE

It was the first day of shooting "Young Man With a Big Horn." I was supposed to appear on the set in a beautiful, low-cut evening gown. I came out, and Michael Curtiz, the director, looked at me, looked at my freckles, and said, "No, no. You'll have to take those spots off." I looked back at him and said, "My freckles are part of me and therefore they are under contract to this studio. And I will not, as you suggest, take them off." I rarely disagree with a director, but I had to then. We ended up compromising with some make-up.

DORIS DAY

I've been outspoken and active in politics in the past, but then I had second thoughts. I think an entertainer has to be extremely conscientious about using his position and popularity as a performer to sway voter decisions. I intend to be active as a voter and a citizen, but not in political rallies. When an entertainer mixes in politics, it may influence voters for the wrong reason. Entertainers just shouldn't plunge in. The wrong man could be elected by the performer's influence.

PAT BOONE

One of my most vivid memories is that, a few years after I got back from the war, I had a couple of pictures that didn't do too well at the box office. I was quite surprised when a magazine writer said that he wanted to do an assignment on me anyway. I answered, "Sure. What's it about?" He said, "We're calling it the Rise and Fall of Jimmy Stewart." I got on the phone to my agent immediately after that, telling him to line up a western for me — quick!

JAMES STEWART

Public life is unbelievable. Being a star means so many things, and all of them opposite normalcy. If your face is familiar, you are stared at, pointed at, laughed at, whispered at, yelled at, and followed. People say lots of things about you that they wouldn't say if they knew you heard. Everything you do well is taken for granted. Any mistake is a matter of great attention.

JOHNNY CASH

I can't be swell-headed with the kind of reviews I've received. Like when I played a Viennese on Broadway in the 1930's. Brooks Atkinson said then, "Stewart was about as Viennese as a cheeseburger." Another critic wrote, "Stewart wandered through the play like a bewildered tourist on the Danube."

JAMES STEWART

Success hasn't affected me much except that I'm a lot more busy and I have a lot more people hollering at me. Of course it also has cut into my family life and ruined my golf game. And people have started coming out of the woodwork. They say "hi" and start talking about the old times. I try not to brush them off. I treat others as I want to be treated.

GLEN CAMPBELL

There are always things happening to keep your ego down to size. One night a lady came backstage and managed to slip into the make-up room. I was being made-up for the cameras. The lady watched all the paints and powders being applied. When it was over, she inspected me closely, and said to my make-up man, "Sir, you are a real genius!"

LAWRENCE WELK

Stardom hasn't changed me, but it has changed people's
attitudes about me. Before, people who wouldn't listen to
me — now they want advice! They wouldn't laugh at my
jokes before — now it's "ha, ha, ha" with a slap on the back.
Well, you learn to weed those people out.

GLEN CAMPBELL

One night when I was in New York, entertaining, I busted
my pants. I bent over to pick up a guitar pick and they busted.
June my wife said the Lord busted my pants. She said I was
entertainin' in high society. And the Lord, to keep me humble
and from flyin' too high from His little ole sky, busted my
pants.

JOHNNY CASH

The wonderful fans I've met during my 50 years in show
business keep saying such nice things to me that I
sometimes worry I may start to believe them. But just about
then, along comes someone who brings me back to earth!
One night on the show we were doing a tag dance and a
large lady, weighing about 220 pounds, came shoving up
from the back of the line, elbowing everyone aside. She
grabbed me around the waist, announcing, "I've never
danced a step in my life. But I always said that if I ever get
to Hollywood, I'd come down and dance on your show."
Well, I've danced with thousands of ladies in my time, but
this lady was something else. I just could not get her on the
beat. Finally, after we struggled for some time on camera,
she pulled back and eyed me with disgust. "You," she said
flatly, "certainly look like a much better dancer on
television."

LAWRENCE WELK

In show business, people seem too often obsessed by the pursuit of fame. They follow it year after year. I have never allowed myself to fall into this trap. And with God's help, my loved ones will escape, too.

GLEN CAMPBELL

A truly successful person should not let that success come between Him and the Lord. And the financial fruits should be shared with Him since success is one of God's many blessings in this life.

DALE EVANS ROGERS

When I gave a Command Performance for the Royal Family in Great Britain, I thought I was a very poised fellow. Standing between Peter Finch and Peter Sellers in the receiving line after the performance, I felt quite in control. But suddenly there was the Queen standing before me, smiling graciously, and all I could think of to say was "Nice to see you here." HERE. Of all things to say! There she was in Buckingham Palace, her own home!

PAT BOONE

Success through any source but Christ is hollow. It cannot last. Only as we surrender ourselves to His total control will we experience the kind of success that will give us the greatest joy — because it is in His Will.

HAL LINDSEY

The demands of success nearly destroyed me. I am dedicating myself to seeing that this neither happens to me again nor to those whose lives I can influence in some way.

JOHNNY CASH

We had been having a hard time on the road one year, and my already shaky self-confidence wasn't being built up at all. I tried hard, but it was all a terrible ordeal. I worried that the audience would laugh in the wrong places, or that I would say the wrong thing. A particular incident at that time stands out in my mind. The management had hired twelve beautiful girls to ride twelve milk-white horses around the edge of the dance floor as part of the evening's entertainment, and one of the horses promptly disgraced himself in the middle of the opening parade. Howls of laughter greeted this performance, and I remember thinking disconsolately, "Well, even the horse is trying to tell me to go back to the farm."

LAWRENCE WELK

We couldn't just take our kids places and be a normal family. When we wanted to go to Disneyland, we were warned that we'd be mobbed. So we disguised ourselves. I put a piece of wadding under my upper lip and wore a mustache and a floppy hat and sloppy clothes. Shirley did her hair in pigtails. And we did the girls up differently. That way we had two terrific days all together.

PAT BOONE

Bob and I feel that our marriage is a success despite the hard times we used to have. But often the difficulties are tests given by God to see how firm our faith, our trust in Him are. My career and Bob's are successful, too, because we have conducted everything in a manner glorifying to the Lord, and he has honored and blessed as a result, giving us fruits we would never have dreamed of years ago.

ANITA BRYANT

Success sure beats pickin' cotton.

GLEN CAMPBELL

Sometimes I wonder if I'm just another one of those guys who do the Jimmy Stewart imitations! I'm a lazy person. By nature I would have planned a quieter life.

JAMES STEWART

At first I resented the lack of privacy in being known. But now I love it, because I love people.

JOHNNY CASH

I'll tell you what I feel about talent. I really feel that nobody can take all the credit for anything. You can't take credit for a voice. It's like giving an avocado an award — it's the same thing. You know, you say, "God, this is a super avocado." Now, are you going to give it an award? It had nothing to do with being super, did it? It's just there when we come in.

DORIS DAY

The first time I got a standing ovation as a performer, I thought they were all getting up to leave.

GLEN CAMPBELL

VALUES

*Pat Boone Anita Bryant James Stewart
Billy Graham Johnny Cash Norman Vincent Peale
Glen Campbell Marjorie Holmes Lawrence Welk
Doris Day Eugenia Price Hal Lindsey
Dale Evans Rogers*

Values which are worth anything come from God. He tells us in His Word how He prefers that we conduct ourselves — and these are the real values in life, because they come from the creator of the human race.

JAMES STEWART

It's wrong to go through life trying to prove something. I think that's where all this stupid competition comes in. It's wrong to feel this way; it makes life miserable.

DORIS DAY

. . . we should plan our lives as though we will be here our full life expectancy, but live as though Christ may come today. We shouldn't drop out of school or worthwhile activities, or stop working, or rush marriage, or any such thing unless Christ clearly leads us to do so. However, we should make the most of our time that is not taken up with the essentials.

HAL LINDSEY

You never work a day when at the end of it you're not a little better than you were in the morning.

LAWRENCE WELK

My family had heard about whiskey and wild women in Hollywood, but they figured I'd come out all right.

GLEN CAMPBELL

Until we can think, and do think, we are second-hand people. Echoes. Imitators, not using our own God-given intelligence. We all need an education.

PAT BOONE

I think the young people are right — we haven't done too much good in this world. If men are still fighting and killing each other, we haven't come all that far. This is what today's young people want to eliminate. That's why they're saying "we want to love". They're absolutely right. We'll never have brotherly love in this world until we stop war. As long as war goes on, it's a glaring example either that we have failed to communicate that, or we're motivated by greed. Well, the young people aren't, and I love them for it.

DORIS DAY

I always follow my Daddy's advice: "Son, believe half of what you see and none of what you hear, and you'll get along in the world!"

GLEN CAMPBELL

All of us have a certain sensitivity. But fortunately, with age comes a little more understanding. A mellowness breaks through the wall of hurt feelings we build up through the years.

LAWRENCE WELK

I was raised in a little shack, learned to pick cotton and work the ground. When you live close to the earth, you learn to understand the basic things about love and hate and what people want from life.

JOHNNY CASH

I try to live for today. The Good Lord will take care of tomorrow.

GLEN CAMPBELL

I think the movie industry is so polluted and degenerate that it's making the whole audience today a group of Peeping Toms. All the fine entertainers today are having strip contests. I'm no prude. When nudity is a story point that's okay — but not when it's to sell tickets. Every suggestive and lewd film we make is lapped up all over the world as the way life is in America. We're playing right into the hands of the Communists by making predominantly sordid films and projecting a one-sided, vicious image of America. I'm trying my level best to get some clean, wholesome entertainment on the screen.

PAT BOONE

In today's world, real values seem to be going up in smoke. There is corruption everywhere. We need a dose of Christian values on a massive scale.

DALE EVANS ROGERS

I don't know where the Goody Two-Shoes image got started. I'm the image created by my parents, and whatever people think is their problem. So I like ice cream better than scotch. Sue me . . . If people think I'm square, then terrific! I do like old-fashioned values in a world that looks pretty much to me as though it's falling apart, and as long as I stick up for my own little corner of the world, I know God will protect me. Tomorrow will take care of itself. Meanwhile, I have to do something about this lousy world today.

DORIS DAY

I don't believe in swearing or cursing, although I know some good people who curse. I've heard men using four-letter words in front of women, but I would never do that . . . Of course I've also heard some women using four-letter words in front of men.

GLEN CAMPBELL

Parents today have failed their children by not giving them more discipline, love and guidelines. I've been criticized for being too much of a disciplinarian with my band, but I think it contributes to our success.

LAWRENCE WELK

I want my life to be a life of giving. I want to give to my wife, to my family, to people no matter who they are. And I've found that a strange thing happens to a man who gets back his freedom after abandoning all hope of ever having it again. The more I give away, the more I seem to have.

JOHNNY CASH

It's important for me to be both honest and understood. I'll go to any length to clear up a matter — even cancel a business engagement or a meeting with a close friend to clear up things with a stranger.

PAT BOONE

What is happening in America? Where is our sense of moral values? Have we, as a people, sunk so low that the only persons we are interested in reading about and seeing are the harlots and adulterers? No wonder the American home is crumbling.

REV. BILLY GRAHAM

I'm gradually strengthening my will power and self-control. I've fought a few good battles with myself and still have a few to go. But I've won the important ones.

JOHNNY CASH

I like hundreds of different people for hundreds of different reasons. Now and then, I like an individual as much because I don't understand him as because I do. I enjoy challenge and variety.

PAT BOONE

It's a real, real hurt when you first face the fact that people are ridiculing you. But those hardships turn out to be good. They make you strong.

LAWRENCE WELK

I feel that charity should be done very quietly, and you can give where you want to give, and do what you want, but just don't blow your horn about it.

DORIS DAY

I think this business of lowering standards is bad. It's been tried before and it hasn't worked. Kids are now searching for their own Utopia. Well, you can't create your own Utopia, you got to find it yourself. They tried in San Francisco at Haight-Asbury and it turned to disaster. I think we've all kind of had it a little too easy since the second World War . . . The 18- and 20-year old kids today just don't have enough knowledge to solve their problems. They've got legitimate beefs and things have got to be changed, but you ain't gonna git it this way.

GLEN CAMPBELL

Seein' people and letting them see me is where it's at. I don't have a lot of ambitions. Selling a good song is my calling in the world. There's a lot of songs to come.

JOHNNY CASH

I try to get better every day.

GLEN CAMPBELL

I suppose at one time it bothered me to be called square or old-fashioned. When we start out in this profession I think all of us are more sensitive to criticism. As you become more popular, however, you learn that you will always be vulnerable to comic take-offs and the like. But you learn to respect the fact that this is one of the nice things about our good land — that people can express their feelings, favorably or unfavorably, about anyone, no matter who he may be.

LAWRENCE WELK

A couple of years ago, publicity people tried to make me into a new Pat Boone. I kept telling them I didn't want to change my image except to add dimensions as an actor. I was happy enough with the old Pat Boone — with all his imperfections. I had no intention of letting down the people who respected me.

PAT BOONE

I have learned that it's not what you see about a person that's important; it's what's inside them.

DORIS DAY

I've been called "the Hip Hick." I take it as a compliment.

GLEN CAMPBELL

Permissiveness and morality in the United States is very dangerous. You can see it in the crime rate. We've got to get back to Christian principles and a decent moral standard. The trend must be reversed if we are going to save ourselves.

LAWRENCE WELK

We have changed our moral code to fit our behavior instead of changing our behavior to harmonize with our moral code.

REV. BILLY GRAHAM

I'm all-American, and I dig America, and I don't like people who are always putting the country down.

GLEN CAMPBELL

If a man works hard and lives right, he can't hold himself back.

LAWRENCE WELK

I'm a man who can't walk away from anything and leave it unfinished.

PAT BOONE

FELLOWSHIP

Three-fifths of the world live in squalor, misery and hunger. Too long have the privileged few exploited and ignored the underprivileged millions of the world. Our selfishness is at long last catching up with us. Unless we begin to act, to share and to do something about this great army of humanity, God will judge us.

REV. BILLY GRAHAM

I have been through the mill and I have had it, so to speak. But due to the fact that I have a musical family that gets together so well and there is such a nice relation to each other, I would just as soon be with them as with anyone else.

LAWRENCE WELK

Being with people you like and respect is so meaningful. Perhaps you have known some of them most of your life. Having friends around for a pleasant evening is one of life's most cherished joys as far as I am concerned. But when those with me are fellow believers how much greater that joy is, for we know that it will be rekindled, one day, in eternity.

JAMES STEWART

I very firmly believe . . . that I've never met a stranger.

DORIS DAY

All I ever wanted from my life was a certain amount of
security, a little luxury if possible, an education, travel, a
career, and — if I had to settle on two things — my family's
happiness, and the short years I live to be of use to somebody.

PAT BOONE

The greatest joy life can hold for any man is the pleasure of
giving. I like to see people smile and laugh and feel happy.

LAWRENCE WELK

When we lived in the bottoms, there was a Negro family in
the slough and I grew up playing with their kids. In Delight
they weren't allowed on the street after 6 o'clock. I always
used to say, 'Gee, that's not right.' My Daddy raised us to
treat everybody kind and nice. That's the way I see it today.

GLEN CAMPBELL

I don't dislike anyone. We all have our faults and I will not
stand in judgement of others.

DORIS DAY

I don't know what I would do without my Christian friends.
They were there when I really needed them. They brought
me truths from God's Word; they were His instruments,
His channels to me. I love them, and we have many fine
times together, begun and ended in prayer.

JOHNNY CASH

When born-again believers get together, a time of wonderful
fellowship usually comes about. It is a time far more
meaningful than anything the world has to offer.

HAL LINDSEY

I found one thing pretty quick. I couldn't go far wrong . . .
if I honestly tried to practice the Golden Rule, and to
remember that we all have a responsibility to the world in
which we live.

PAT BOONE

I love that special passage from St. Matthew: "Love thy
neighbor as thyself." I think there is great power for good
contained in these simple words. If all of us could learn to
love our neighbors as we do ourselves, we would travel a
long way on the road to universal happiness. For love is
reflected in love. And hatred would soon be driven out.

DORIS DAY

I want to leave something that will help other people. I have
been so lucky . . . so lucky . . . and I would like to help other
people find some of the joy and peace that have been mine.

LAWRENCE WELK

Thank you for my friends, God. And thank you for my
family. Thank you for all the people whose lives mingle with
mine. Sometimes so frantically, causing so many problems,
but sometimes so joyfully, wonderfully too. Sometimes, for
no good reason, my heart just fills up with love for them. I
want to hug them, tell them, show them, stage a kind of
one-dame love demonstration . . . Thank you, God, for these
people.

MARJORIE HOLMES

Most of the world's problems could be solved if people
would learn to see each other's view points.

GLEN CAMPBELL

I enjoy being with *people* but especially believers. We have a bond that is almost indescribable to the unsaved. It comes from the joy of knowing that Christ died for our sins and as a result of our acceptance of Him into our lives as Saviour and Lord, we can go to the grave knowing that existence for us does not end there. This kind of fellowship, in this world and in the next, is a tremendous part of life.

ANITA BRYANT

Christians should never forsake fellowship among themselves. Where two or more are gathered together, God's presence can be felt strongly. How very wonderful it is when believers get together and talk over the things of the Lord. A joyous time indeed!

DALE EVANS ROGERS

I'm not a prejudiced person at all. I think the civil rights thing will take care of itself in time. They're not gonna do it in one night, you know. Rome wasn't built in a day.

GLEN CAMPBELL

When a man takes on a responsibility such as I assumed when I decided that I really want to stay in the music field and really wanted to have an orchestra and singers, then he must understand that he is, to a great extent, responsible for the lives of the people who work with him. And, because I always knew that it was well-known that many musicians — many people in show business — may be less than morally upright, I had to keep remembering that it wasn't enough for me to stay on the straight and narrow. I had to make sure that my people did so, too.

LAWRENCE WELK

I have a concept in business where we develop our own people. We take them at a young age — not as young as we would like because of our child labor laws. I went to Washington to see if I could put my ideas across. Along with training people, we also share profits — 15 percent, which is as much as we are allowed to share, and we share our extra things. I call it a 'family plan.'

LAWRENCE WELK

I'll work my fanny off for animals, because I feel that animals were put here to teach us. I do. Every time I talk about them I could cry. They're not competitive, and not greedy and not vicious. Nothing . . . nothing. No hang-ups . . . you know, a pat on the head and a little food, and that's all. It's beautiful, they're really beautiful.

DORIS DAY

THE WORD

*Pat Boone Anita Bryant James Stewart
Billy Graham Johnny Cash Norman Vincent Peale
Glen Campbell Marjorie Holmes Lawrence Welk
Doris Day Eugenia Price Hal Lindsey
Dale Evans Rogers*

A man should never be afraid to speak out for what he believes. Sometimes he may be considered narrow-minded but better to be narrow-minded than broad-minded and in the control of Satan.

GLEN CAMPBELL

"Soul-saving" is all but a lost art in many churches. Indeed, it is a sad fact that in not a few churches not a single soul is spiritually changed in a year or in five years for that matter. In fact, laymen tell me that some preachers even regard soul-saving as, shall we say, corny. I cannot believe that such an attitude could exist in evangelical Christianity — a form of faith and spiritual practice which has always sought to save the souls of individuals through the power of God and the sacrificial death and resurrection of Jesus Christ. And sadly enough along with decline in spiritual faith some of our freedoms also suffer curtailment.

DR. NORMAN VINCENT PEALE

I think all teenagers should make out their own check lists for maturity. And their guideposts in adult life should be: the Bible, the Golden Rule, cleanliness is next to godliness, and sound financial practices.

PAT BOONE

My church is the Church of Christ. It's a simple fundamentalist organization. Our aim is to add nothing in the way of tradition which is not explicitly authorized in the New Testament. Our idea is bare, basic simplicity; by adding or subtracting something to suit yourself, you lose something. For me, my belief has caused me to make decisions that might seem absurd to other people, but I based them on what I thought was good for my family and my relationship to God, not my career.

PAT BOONE

Every person is an individual and every unsaved person has to be treated as an individual, and approached differently from all others. If you don't approach these people correctly you will not only turn them off toward yourself, but also for future witnesses — and maybe even forever.

ANITA BRYANT

I have never been one to stand over people and say to them that they *have* to believe in that or that. But if people do come to me with minds that are confused, I try my best to present to them a picture of the peace that God can bestow . . . if they let Him do so.

DORIS DAY

We need Christ in every phase of our lives. Christ must be taken out into the marketplace, into our halls of learning, into our legislative assemblies. Christ must be taken to Africa, where a continent is being engulfed in an inferno of changes. Christ must be taken to Asia, where people are starving not only for food but for a fuller and richer way of life.

REV. BILLY GRAHAM

Some traditional churches have learned to provide the personal ministry of God's truth to the youth and you will find their youth departments are flourishing. But they are the exception, unfortunately. Most churches seem to be on the wrong wave length altogether. Some have the truth, but can't communicate it to today's youth; others simply don't teach the truth, and though they try "underground church" approaches, they can't compete with the radical political organizations. Many youth are going to be on the front edge of a movement toward first century-type Christianity, with an emphasis upon people and their needs rather than buildings and unwieldy programs.

HAL LINDSEY

Every believer should be a missionary, proclaiming the message of salvation. Not all of us can go to foreign fields but those of us who remain behind should witness to those around us. Our very lives should be a living testimony to the reality and the control of Almighty God.

DALE EVANS ROGERS

Witnessing makes you complete. God gave me a burden, and until I was able to sow in tears I wasn't able to reap in joy.

ANITA BRYANT

My kids ask me questions about God. Like they ask, "Where does God live?" And I say, "Well, He lives in Heaven." And then they say, "Where's Heaven?" And I say, "Well, honeys, heaven is a place where you go if you've done good while you're living on earth. So be nice to other people. Be polite. Be considerate. And have faith in your fellow man."

GLEN CAMPBELL

My conduct is my testimony. If people can see God, somehow, through me, then I will be satisfied. I go to a great many places and meet thousands of people. And if God can use me to touch their lives in a special way, then I am happy.

LAWRENCE WELK

There are many instances of Christians who prayed for years for the salvation of a family member. Meanwhile, I would think, their day-by-day walk in the faith witnessed to their sincerity towards the Lord.

ANITA BRYANT

The new generation has rejected materialism and is ripe for different experiences then owning things or being owned by their things. Young people have discovered that drugs, group sex, anti-social and anti-establishment behavior have all ended in grief. I think the Jesus movement is real and legitimate, and that the kids turning to it are being saved.

PAT BOONE

And there is that word *communicate*. God has bid us come — all of us. Are we letting this be known? I don't mean are we standing on platforms giving high pressure "invitations" while the congregation sings "Just As I Am." I mean are we communicating the heart of God? Are we daring to let Him show us how wide His love really is? Are we courageous enough to be willing to be misunderstood as we speak out of the caring He has placed in our hearts . . . More and more I am convinced that I can communicate what I really believe about the poured-out life of God on His cross by permitting His love to change me in the wellsprings of my being.

EUGENIA PRICE

I have never been hesitant to speak out for what I believe. I think people are often too timid. But having the strength of your convictions is very important, especially today. God saw me through much that could have been fatal during the Second World War, and I would be hypocritical if I didn't tell others about Him.

JAMES STEWART

We tend to reach and plead and try to persuade people to commit their lives to Christ. This is holy ground on which we tread, and we dare not stamp around on it insensitively in our zeal for numbers we can boast about! People cannot be persuaded by other people to commit their lives. The person with the life in hand must do this — alone with God.

EUGENIA PRICE

Keep the faith. It's the best witness you've got going for you.

ANITA BRYANT

If all churches were engaged in perennial evangelism, I don't think there would ever be need for a person like me.

REV. BILLY GRAHAM

My gospel film was one of my ways of spreading the Word. Sometimes, the way we conduct ourselves spreads the Word, also, and causes it *not* to be spread, even to be hurt. I give my money back to missionary efforts dedicated to the cause of Christ. As the Bible teaches us, the Word should be spread to the furthermost corners of this old earth.

JOHNNY CASH

ACKNOWLEDGEMENTS

The compiler and the publisher have made every effort to trace the ownership of all copyrighted material and to secure permission from copyright holders of such material. In the event of any question arising as to the use of any material the compiler and the publisher, while expressing regret for inadvertent error, will be pleased to make the necessary corrections in future printings. Grateful acknowledgment is made for the use of the following material:

DOUBLEDAY & COMPANY, INC., for excerpts from *I've Got to Talk to Somebody, God,* by Marjorie Holmes, copyright © 1968 by Marjorie Holmes; from *Nobody Else Will Listen* by Marjorie Holmes, copyright © 1969 by Marjorie Holmes; from *A Guide to Self-Control* by Norman Vincent Peale, copyright © 1965 by Norman Vincent Peale.

DROKE HOUSE PUBLISHERS, INC., for excerpts from *The Quotable Billy Graham,* copyright © 1966, by Droke Publishers, Inc.

PRENTICE-HALL, INC., for excerpts from *The Tough-Minded Optimist* by Norman Vincent Peale, copyright © 1961; from *The Amazing Results of Positive Thinking* by Norman Vincent Peale, copyright © 1959; from *Wunnerful, Wunnerful* by Lawrence Welk, copyright © 1971. *All material copyright Prentice-Hall, Inc.*

FLEMING H. REVELL COMPANY for excerpts from *Mine Eyes Have Seen the Glory* by Anita Bryant, copyright © 1970; from *Amazing Grace* by Anita Bryant, copyright © 1971; from *Bless This House* by Anita Bryant, copyright © 1972; from *Fishers of Men* by Anita Bryant, copyright © 1973; from *To My Son* by Dale Evans Rogers, copyright © 1957; from *No Two Ways About It*